The Book of

THE BOOK OF REFLECTION

Published by Arcturus Publishing Limited,
1-7 Shand Street, London SE1 2ES.

First published 2000.
This edition printed 2001.

©Text The School of Economic Science.
©Design Arcturus Publishing Limited.

Typeset by Christopher Smith Design.
Printed in Hong Kong.

The Book of

REFLECTION

Introduction

The purpose of 'Reflection' is a simple one: release - release from the confines and constraints that hold us all in check; release from tension and anxiety, release from dullness of mind and heaviness of heart.

This is a book about self discovery. It provides a practical path in ten stages to transform the way you meet events, no longer at the mercy of exterior forces but in touch with the essential presence that lies at the heart of experience, the profound core of consciousness that illuminates it all.

These simple steps will enable you to meet life in an altogether more open, philosophical and compassionate way. They will help you to discover life's inherent beauty, its simplicity and profundity.

Divided into ten stages, with seven reflections for each stage, 'Reflection' provides a day by day programme to support the course of practical philosophy from which it arose. It springs directly from the material considered in the classes and will help to build on the discoveries made there, but whether attending a class or not, what is to be found in the book provides a source of continuing inspiration.

Use it as a practical tool. Carry it with you and refer to it regularly. Whatever you face in life, what is to be found in 'Reflection' is of immense and immediate benefit.

If you wish to discover more about practical philosophy phone The School of Economic Science on 020 7835 1256.

Finding peace in the present

At the heart of these ten stages in the development of a more reflective attitude to life is a simple and yet powerful practice. This practice allows you not only to connect fully with all those demands that life continually lays upon you, but also to reflect the still light of consciousness which illuminates it all.

The practice can be undertaken anywhere and at any time regardless of your circumstances, at times of quiet and in the midst of action. It can be practised for any length of time, for two minutes or more. Even a single moment has its merit.

Come into the present by leaving concerns for past and future. Fall still, and let go all physical tension. Connect mind with the senses.

And be aware of the beauty around you.
See colour and form. Let listening be wide.
Go beyond the surface of sensory impression.
Become conscious of the underlying silence and space.

Rest in the peace of the present.

And then, having found rest, move on to the next activity, meeting the moment, moment by moment.

Stage One

Stage One

Why be wise?

'...to thine own self be true'

Stage One

1. PHILO - SOPHY
Love of Wisdom

Consider those you think wise.

What qualities do they possess?

Look out for the signs of wisdom in those around you.

Notice both their knowledge and their love.

2. 'Knowledge arises from experience not information.'
Reflect on events, and consider what they are
telling you.

True philosophy is a practical matter.
Knowledge meets you moment
by moment.

Make sure you're
there when it
happens.

3. *'This above all: to thine own self be true.'*

What does it mean in any situation to remain true to yourself, and what might lead you into falsehood?

4. What is the practical purpose of gaining wisdom?

Ask yourself how you might act wisely in the situation you are facing now?

Hold true to the ideal of Wisdom.

5. *Full many a glorious morning have I seen*
   Flatter the mountain-tops with sovereign eye,
   Kissing with golden face the meadows green,
   Gilding pale streams with heavenly alchemy.

SONNET 33 SHAKESPEARE

Here's a description of beauty. Consider your view of the world. How does it differ from Shakespeare's?

> *If it appears something less than his,*
> *open the mind to new possibilities.*

6. To be conscious means to know all together.

Be aware of your own view.

Don't always be content with the way you habitually see things.

Consider an alternative.

Adopt a wider view.

7. How much of the day do you spend transferred to another place and another time?

When you catch yourself hanging 'Back in five minutes' on the door, take it down, and enter the here and now.

PASSAGE FOR
REFLECTION.

This above all: to thine own self be true,
And it must follow, as the night the day,
Thou canst not then be false to any man.

SHAKESPEARE: 'HAMLET'

Remember the practice of finding peace in the present.

Stage Two

Finding Freedom

*'...embracing all living creatures
and the whole of nature in its beauty.'*

Stage Two

1. *Learn to be wise not after the event but at the time.*

Ask yourself what you might offer the moment rather than what you can take from it.

2. *'He tastes nothing who has not tasted for himself.'*

What does wisdom taste like?

TASTING FOR YOURSELF:
> *Reflect on the reflections.*
> *Practise the practices.*
> *Observe the results,*
> *Remember those who served wisdom with*
> *their whole heart. Wisdom not only*
> *requires intellectual understanding*
> *but also emotional commitment*
> *and practice, above all practice.*

3. *Observe the nature of confining thought in form of:*
    preoccupations,
    unreasonable likes and dislikes,
    habitual responses
    and emotional tendencies.

   Lift your mind above confining thought.

   Look up.

        See the beauty and find the
           simple solution.

4. *The more we go deep the more we are aware. Rather than being driven across the surface of life, employ the Practice to dip below the surface, to make a more profound connection with life.*

It more than repays the time spent, with a greater awareness of how best to meet the demands of the day.

Do it on the wing.

Be inventive.

5. *It is impossible to grow in wisdom bound by fear and anxiety.*

It is impossible to live a healthy and active life racked by stress.

Come into the moment. Connect with colour and form, light and space.

Let go of emotional confines and touch the underlying stillness.

6. *Don't think the demands are too demanding to contemplate contemplation.*

When the pressures are most insistent, don't cling on the tighter, but instead connect with your own inner calm.

7. *And having gained that inner connection, turn out and give yourself to the immediate need, for:*

> *by giving we receive,*
>
> *by as much as we overcome confining thought so we discover our own inner resources.*

PASSAGE FOR REFLECTION.

A human being is part of the whole, called by us "Universe", a part limited in time and space. He experiences himself, his thoughts and feelings as something separated from the rest - a kind of optical delusion of his consciousness. This delusion is a kind of prison for us, restricting us to our personal desires and to affection for a few persons nearest to us. Our task must be to free ourselves from this prison by widening our circle of compassion to embrace all living creatures and the whole of nature in its beauty.

ALBERT EINSTEIN

Stage Three

Living in the Light

'I must first know myself.'

Stage Three

1. If you find life whirling through your· mind, turning into a jumble of events, bring some measure to the confusion.

Draw your sentences to an end before rushing onto the next.

Punctuate your life with the Practice.

2. Notice how you are prompted by desire, either your own or somebody else's.

Rather than being driven ever onward by its power, bring an element of rest to the pressure of events.

Pause before pressing on.

DESIRE > ...REST... DESIRE >

Notice what effect this practice has on the way you deal with the stress of life.

3. We think we can act, but contemplation is another matter. Pressure creates tension - tension creates stress - stress creates disease.

Contemplation creates calm and calm dissolves disease.

ACTION > ...CONTEMPLATION... ACTION >

Live contemplatively as well as actively.

4. *Count your blessings.*

Look at those things for which you should be grateful, and the next time you find yourself bewailing your lot, learn to value those things that habit makes you overlook.

5.

We talk about winning people's hearts and minds and loving someone body and soul. Consider how we divide ourselves up into three parts: HEAD, HEART, BODY. Notice how they have their different demands and how the power of Reason brings those conflicting demands into harmony. Use the Practice to connect with the light of consciousness, the source of everything reasonable.

6. *Observe bodily movement.*

Notice changes in your emotional state.

Detect movements of the mind.

Reflect upon that which has the power to observe these changes rather than being controlled by what at any moment commands the mind.

7. *See how the attention operates.*

Notice what you are captured by, and, at the moment you are about to be sucked in, stay with the light that illuminates everything that comes before the mind.

This is the Light of Consciousness.

It is cool, calm and collected.

**PASSAGE FOR
REFLECTION.**

I must first know myself, as the
Delphian inscription says; to be
curious of that which is not my
concern, while I am in ignorance of
my own self would be ridiculous.

PLATO: PHAEDRUS 229 E

Our general instinct to seek and learn,
our longing to possess ourselves of
whatsoever is lovely in the vision, will
set us inquiring into the nature of the
instrument with which we search.

PLOTINUS THE ENNEADS IV iii. 1

Jesus said: Whosoever knows the All
but fails to know himself lacks
everything.

THE GOSPEL ACCORDING TO THOMAS, LOG .3

Seek for self knowledge. It is the essential purpose of life.

Stage Four

In Touch with the Unchanging

'...this state of soul is called wisdom.'

Stage Four

1. If tension arises, look to its cause.

Notice the determined individual within you who wants to wrench things to some preconceived end.

2. *Be there when the event takes place.*

*Listen, really listen, to what is
forthcoming in the here
and now.*

*Let that determine
your decision.*

3. *Cultivate awareness through concentration.*

Cultivate relaxation by letting go.

4. *The way to meet the need of the moment is discovered in the moment by responding flexibly, intelligently and without preconception.*

5. There is no life than the life that is being lived now. Freedom lies in being there when it happens. Look for the perfection in the present moment.

| First stage | Second stage |

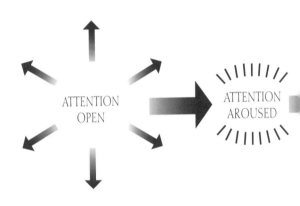

ATTENTION OPEN

ATTENTION AROUSED

6. When your attention is aroused and focussed, rememb
the observer as well as that which is drawing you in.
This acknowledgment leads you to the still point in a wo
of constant change.

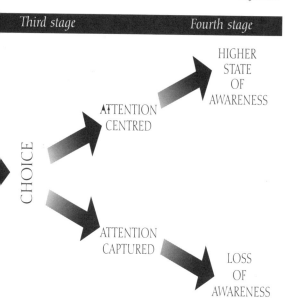

HIGHER
STATE
OF
AWARENESS

ATTENTION
CENTRED

CHOICE

ATTENTION
CAPTURED

LOSS
OF
AWARENESS

7. *Peace and clarity come when attention is centred rather than being completely caught by those conflicting demands and desires that usually command our minds.*

**PASSAGE FOR
REFLECTION**.

*When she (the Soul) contemplates
in herself and by herself, then she
passes into another world, the region
of purity and eternity, and
immortality, and unchangeableness,
which are her kindred, and with
them she ever lives, when she is by
herself and is not let or hindered;
then she ceases from her erring
ways, and being in communion
with the unchanging is unchanging.
And this state of soul is called
wisdom.*

PLATO: THE 'PHAEDO'

*Discover the unchanging through the Practice, and remain
centred rather than being at the mercy of events.
This is a sure way to wisdom.*

Stage Five

Being Aware of Beauty

*'Its beauty shines
in every individual thing.'*

Stage Five

1. There is nothing like beauty to encourage connection with the senses.

Fortunately Nature is not short of it.

Look out for the signs of beauty everywhere.

2. Look out for something beautifully done.

Do something beautiful yourself.

Perform a simple action with care and attention.

3. Notice how love and beauty are so closely linked.

What's in the nature of people you know who may not possess any obvious signs of physical beauty but have some inner quality that shines through?

How do they treat others?

How do they respond to life?

4. *What of our capability for appreciating beauty?*

How could we appreciate beauty without if there were no beauty within?

'The physical forms look beautiful because the mind is beautiful.'

Every time you recognise the beauty without you testify to the beauty within.

5. Train the mind to look with the eye of the artist.

Don't automatically overlook those things that come before the senses, but look again with care.

Don't let life pass unnoticed.

6. *Appreciate great ideas. Taste them like you would fine food.*

Give them time so they can be properly appreciated.

Enjoy their beauty to the full.

7. *The recognition of beauty without stimulates the principle of beauty within, which in turn encourages the appreciation of beauty everywhere.*

When something of beauty is discovered stay with the inner experience that arises in response to beauty.

Let that knowledge continue to inform your thought.

Act from that.

PASSAGE FOR REFLECTION.

It was the chief work of the divine Plato ... to reveal the principle of unity in all things, which is called appropriately the One itself. He also asserted that in all things there is one truth, that is the light of the One itself ... which is poured into all minds and forms, presenting the forms to the minds and joining the minds to the forms.

Whoever wishes to profess the study of Plato should therefore honour the one truth ... Its splendour shines in every individual thing according to its nature and is called grace and beauty; and where it shines more clearly, it especially attracts those who are watching, stimulates those who think, and catches and possesses those who draw near to it.

THE LETTERS OF MARSILIO FICINO VOL. 1

Look out for the light of beauty.

Stage Six

Serenity of Mind

'If there were no beauty in the observer,
then he would not find beauty outside.'

Stage Six

1. What is your state of awareness?

How keenly do you appreciate
things now?

What can you do to make a step
towards a greater state of wakefulness?

When in the thrall of all those
thoughts and emotions which
usually captivate heart and
mind, don't accept them as the
only possibility.

Be wise now, not at some other time,
even if 'now' doesn't appear too encouraging.

2. When the mind is dull and heavy and the heart cold and closed, don't accept this as inevitable.

Don't think that what you are experiencing at present is who you really are. Instead of getting lost in your current state of heart and mind, look out.

See what the situation is asking of you, and if you can't think where to begin, start with the nearest thing to hand.

3. *When agitation rules, and your mind is restless, and your heart is seething with emotion, and you feel totally under pressure, come to stillness.*

> *Look out and let it go.*

> *Find rest in the midst of action.*

> *Give yourself to the present need.*

> *And when tensions return keep letting go.*

4. *Be aware of these states that rule the heart, mind and body.*

Notice how the balance of these states undergoes constant change.

There are times when dullness and inertia predominates and other times a restless frustration, and then, as if by grace, clarity and contentment arises.

All may be experienced.

By quiet observation, find balance and harmony, and then act according to the need rather than being ruled by any prevailing quality of heart and mind.

5. Connect with beauty.

'Its splendour shines in every individual thing according to its nature.'

The appreciation of beauty leads to serenity of mind.

Serenity of mind leads to a greater appreciation of beauty

One leads automatically to the other.

6. *Rather than be possessed by agitation and anxiety, recover your radiance by letting go. Rest with the still light of consciousness which remains unaffected by the stress of life. And having found rest, act from there.*

7. *Rather than chasing after all those things that appear to lie out there, seeking to find an elusive satisfaction in things that come to pass, connect instead with the essential thing, the consciousness that empowers it all.*

That is the source of true fulfillment, happiness and peace.

**PASSAGE FOR
REFLECTION**.

Beauty is reflected in the objects and
in the observers who receive the
beauty through the objects. If there
were no beauty in the observer, then
he would not find beauty outside.
The mere fact that beauty is seen
proves that there is beauty already
present in the being of the observer.
Nowhere in creation does beauty
stand by itself. The physical or
sensory beauty has its foundations
in the mental or subtle realm.
The physical forms look beautiful
because the mind is beautiful.

SHANTANAND SARASWATI

Stage Seven

Self Remembering

'...waken in yourself that other vision,
the birthright of all'

Stage Seven

1. Communion means coming together as one. Inner communion indicates a returning home to the centre of one's being.

To live in knowledge of that makes communion with others possible.

It encourages connection of all kinds; therefore connect within and without.

2. Changing our minds is a far more common occurrence than we would ever suspect.

Sometimes we change moment by moment: totally confident in ourselves one moment, thrown into confusion the next.

Think of the changes of heart and mind you experience continuously.

Amidst all this change, stay true to your true identity, the still centre of consciousness.

3. Who can fail to observe the body moving?

Who can fail to observe the mind thinking?

Who can fail to observe the heart being overwhelmed by emotion?

To free yourself from identification with any of the states you might encounter, there is a simple and utterly reasonable formula: 'I am not that which I can observe.'

Remember these words when you are about to become embroiled.

4. To directly confront those constraints that confine us to a limited perception of things, within ourselves or without, we can say of it: "Not this, not this."

> Useful words to employ when
> negative emotion rises.

5. *Wisdom is dependent on the level of being.*

*The level of being is dependent on
self remembering.*

*Self remembering is dependent on overcoming
self forgetting.*

*Self forgetting is overcome by
breaking the bonds of limitation.*

6. Simple beauty is discovered in simple things.

Don't dismiss anything as 'unworthy'.

7. *Above all don't dismiss yourself as 'unworthy'.*

Of those ideas we hold about ourselves, this is the most damaging.

There is a beauty in self belief, not born out of pride, but out of simplicity, the simple experience that within us all there is something constant and true, regardless of what self doubt might, at any particular moment, possess the mind.

PASSAGE FOR REFLECTION.

> *You must close the eyes
> and waken in yourself
> that other vision, the
> birthright of all, but
> which few turn to use.*

> *PLOTINUS*

Use the Practice to discover your birthright.

Stage Eight

Inner Contentment

*'Nowhere can a man find a quieter
or more untroubled retreat
than in his own soul'*

Stage Eight

1. It's a matter of balance and measure.

Look at those things which habitually get you wrong footed.

Find your feet by abandoning emotional identification.

Find measure by doing nothing in excess.

2. Notice the ever changing balance of those psychological states that rule heart and body as well as mind.

By observing their movements, allow the balance and measure to be maintained, everything suited to the demands of the moment.

When action is needed, act, when calm is needed be calm, when rest is needed, sleep.

By observation find the proper measure for all these things.

Be aware when the measure is exceeded.

3. Be conscious of how the light of consciousness illuminates the mind and how everything that comes before the mind is empowered by that light.

When the power is withdrawn these things are no longer fed.

Therefore, when negative emotion rules the mind, withdraw the light.

Lend your attention to something constructive.

THE CAPABILITY
OF DECIDING TRUTH
FROM UNTRUTH

4.

Rather than allowing agitation and preoccupation to decide the truth or untruth of anything, let the thing itself be presented to the still mind. Let it be judged on its own merits.

5. To thine own self be true. - William Shakespeare.

Find enduring satisfaction not so much by reaching out after the objects of satisfaction but by entering ever more deeply into that which grants satisfaction, your own centre of stillness and certainty. Be true to that.

6. *He who kisses the Joy as it flies lives in Eternity's sunrise. - William Blake*

When you turn out to face the flow of life, rather than clinging on to all the claims, kiss life as it flies.

Find your pleasure in what the moment offers, and then, having embraced that moment, simply let it go.

7. *Claim nothing. Enjoy.*

PASSAGE FOR REFLECTION.

Men seek seclusion in the wilderness, by the seashore, or in the mountains - a dream you have cherished only too fondly yourself. But such fancies are wholly unworthy of a philosopher, since at any moment you choose you can retire within yourself. Nowhere can a man find a quieter or more untroubled retreat than in his own soul; above all, he who possesses resources within himself, which he need only contemplate to secure immediate ease of mind . Avail yourself often then, of this retirement, and so continually renew yourself.

MARCUS AURELIUS MEDITATIONS

Stage Nine

Living Life Afresh

'...the gladness that transfigures the face of man.'

Stage Nine

1. *No effort in this work
is ever wasted.*

*Any attempt to make a step
on the path of wisdom, regardless
of the difficulty encountered, is
never a failure.*

2. Eternity's sunrise doesn't occur every 24 hours, but in every moment.

The present is always lit. Be conscious of the present.

3. Meet people afresh, not sentenced by the ideas you hold about them, but determined to greet them as if for the first time.

4. *Don't spend your time in the archives of past impressions and petty anxieties.*

Being bound to these two burdens can so easily remove all the novelty from life, destroy its freshness and vitality.

5. *The light of reason illuminates the present.*

Fear exists when projecting the past into the future.

6. Give up those deep rooted ideas you hold about yourself.

How can we properly attend to what lies before us when peered at through a screen of self concern?

7 Ask yourself what you are serving in any situation: the personal interest or the greater whole.

One leads to contraction, separation and isolation.

The other leads to a greater awareness of an ever expanding reality.

PASSAGE FOR REFLECTION.

Our minds are not apart from the world..
..The harmony and beauty of the face of Nature, is at root one with the gladness that transfigures the face of man.

ARTHUR EDDINGTON

Every object clearly seen, opens up a new object of perception in us.

GOETHE

Stage Ten

The Truth About Ourselves

*'Out of Self comes the breath
that is the life of all things.'*

Stage Ten

1. Every moment has its value, and its value increases according to the degree of consciousness we bring to it.

By learning to value the moment, we inevitably become more conscious of the moment and its own particular beauty.

2. *Discrimination is not only to do with dividing things up in an ever more searching analysis; discrimination is also to do with remembering the unity in diversity.*

3. *If we remember the whole, the parts will naturally find their place and measure.*

What does 'to remember' involve after all but a putting back together of the dismembered parts and a realisation of the whole.

4. When things seem to be falling apart, then is the time to make a particularly conscious attempt to return to the still centre, and when you have done that, ask yourself whether what you are bent on will tend to integrate or disintegrate.

5. However it might manifest in the moment, continue to pursue the journey from individual to universal, for in truth the individual is universal.

Every time, therefore, we make a move away from the limited and divided so we experience something of the truth about ourselves.

6. Nothing is more central to any experience than the consciousness that grants us that experience.

Learn to rejoice in the evidence of that consciousness, whether it be in the movement of a distant star or the opening of a child's eyes.

And when you feel your own vitality, acknowledge the consciousness within.

7. Contentment comes from self knowledge, and happiness is the mark of a conscious life.

By being happy in yourself, let that happiness spread.

This is how to live in harmony with others.

PASSAGE FOR REFLECTION.

> The Self is one. Unmoving it moves;
> faster than the mind. The senses lag,
> but Self runs ahead. Unmoving it
> outruns pursuit. Out of Self comes
> the breath that is the life of all things.
> Unmoving, it moves; is far away, yet
> near; within all, outside all.
> Of a certainty the man who can see
> all creatures in himself, himself in all
> creatures, knows no sorrow.

EESHA UPANISHAD

Seek out the uniting factor. Act from that.

Final Thought

You have here a tool for use, and, if you do refer to it regularly, no further justification for its use will be required. The results will speak for themselves.

In a world where division and separation can be our usual experience, a method which reminds us of life's unifying factor, our own underlying consciousness, is of supreme importance.

Allow what is to be found in this book to help you connect with that.